KU-421-703

CONTENTS

FOREWORD

I'm always on the lookout for new ways to tell Bible stories. That's what storytellers do. The hardest job is finding a compelling and original "way in" to a story. And when I find something that works, I get really excited.

My grandchildren are mad keen on Minecraft ®. They don't get much game-playing time, but when they do, Minecraft ® is their first choice. The older two (nine and six) love building the worlds, while the youngest, who is only three, simply enjoys digging holes and getting stuck in them.

So when I showed them a few sample pages from *The Unofficial Bible for Minecrafters* their responses ranged from "It's funny" (which it is!) to "When can I read some more?"

As for me, I turned the pages just to see what the creators of the book would get up to next and how they would bring each scene to Minecrafter-life. And I have to say that I was surprised and delighted.

Every now and then, someone comes up with a new way of telling Bible stories that is just that little bit different. And if this is a "way in" for someone (and there are thousands of Minecrafters out there) and it's compelling, intriguing, and faithful to the text, then I'm happy to recommend it. That's what storytellers do.

Bob Hartman

Bob Hartman, Storyteller

$10
C4

THE UNOFFICIAL

BIBLE FOR MINECRAFTERS

THE CROSS AND THE MIRACLE

GARRETT ROMINES AND CHRISTOPHER MIKO

STORIES FROM THE BIBLE TOLD BLOCK BY BLOCK

LION

This book is not authorized or sponsored by Microsoft Corporation, Mojang AB, Notch Development AB, or Scholastic Corporation, or any other person or entity owning or controlling rights in the Minecraft name, trademark, or copyrights.

Text copyright © 2016 Christopher Miko and Garrett Romines
Illustrations copyright © 2016 Christopher Miko and Garrett Romines
This mini edition copyright © 2018 Lion Hudson IP Limited

The right of Christopher Miko and Garrett Romines to be identified as the authors and illustrators of this work has been asserted by them in accordance with the Copyright, Designs and Patents Act 1988.

All rights reserved. No part of this publication may be reproduced or transmitted in any form or by any means, electronic or mechanical, including photocopy, recording, or any information storage and retrieval system, without permission in writing from the publisher.

Published by
Lion Hudson Limited
Wilkinson House, Jordan Hill Business Park,
Banbury Road, Oxford OX2 8DR, England
www.lionhudson.com

ISBN 978 0 7459 7740 9

Original Bible edition published by Sky Pony Press, 307 West 36th Street, 11th Floor, New York, NY 10018

Stories originally published in *The Unofficial Old Testament for Minecrafters* and *The Unofficial New Testament for Minecrafters* 2016
This mini edition 2018

Acknowledgments
A catalogue record for this book is available from the British Library
Minecraft ® is a registered trademark of Notch Development AB.
The Minecraft ® game is copyright © Mojang AB.

Printed and bound in China, June 2018, LH54

JESUS GOES TO JERUSALEM
Matthew 21

God, Jesus is off to Jerusalem!

hat's right! Jesus is ready
nd.

The end?

Go into the village that is just ahead, and you will find a donkey tied to a post. Untie it and bring it to me.

THE TIME OF PASSOVER WAS APPROACHING, AND JESUS AND HIS DISCIPLES WERE ON THEIR WAY TO JERUSALEM. JESUS TOLD TWO OF HIS DISCIPLES TO GO ON AHEAD TO THE NEAREST VILLAGE.

THIS WAS FORETOLD THROUGH THE PROPHET, WHO SAID: "LOOK — YOUR KING IS COMING TO YOU... RIDING ON A DONKEY."

THE DISCIPLES FOUND A DONKEY EXACTLY AS JESUS HAD DESCRIBED.

THEY PUT SOME CLOTHES OVER ITS BACK. THEN JESUS SAT ON IT.

PEOPLE FROM ALL AROUND RUSHED TO GREET JESUS.

HE TRIUMPHANTLY ENTERED JERUSALEM. PEOPLE LAID THEIR CLOAKS AND PALM LEAVES ON THE GROUND BEFORE HIM.

SOME OF THE CROWD WONDERED WHO HE WAS.
Who is he?
This is Jesus of Nazareth!

JESUS IN JERUSALEM
Matthew 21–23

Now it's time for my Son to
challenge the authorities.

ONCE JESUS ENTERED THE CITY, HE MADE HIS WAY TO THE TEMPLE. HE WAS FILLED WITH OUTRAGE AT WHAT HE SAW: THERE WERE MONEY CHANGERS AND PEOPLE BUYING AND SELLING WARES IN ORDER TO MAKE A PROFIT. JESUS GRABBED A ROPE.

HE DROVE OUT ALL WHO WERE BUYING AND SELLING THERE.

LATER, THE BLIND AND THE LAME CAME TO JESUS AT THE TEMPLE, AND HE HEALED THEM. THE CHIEF PRIESTS AND TEACHERS OF THE LAW WERE INDIGNANT WHEN THEY HEARD CHILDREN PRAISING JESUS.

Teacher, we know that you are
a man of integrity and that you
teach the way of God. Tell us,
is it right to pay taxes to the
Roman emperor or not?

You hypocrites! Show me a coin.

Whose image
is on this
coin? And
whose name?

The emperor's.

Then give the emperor
what belongs to the
emperor and to God
what belongs to God.

10

THEY BROUGHT HIM A COIN AND
HE ASKED THEM A QUESTION.

You must be careful to do everything they tell you. But do not behave in the way they do, for they do not always practise what they preach.

JESUS GAVE THE CROWD AND HIS DISCIPLES A WARNING ABOUT THE PHARISEES AND THE TEACHERS OF THE LAW.

Everything they do is done for people to see: they love the place of honour at banquets and the most important seats in the synagogues; they love to be called "Teacher" by others.

You are not to be called "Teacher", for you have one teacher. For those who make themselves great will be humbled, and those who humble themselves will be made great.

JESUS' FINAL DAYS

Matthew 26–27; Luke 23

The crucial moment has arrived. My plan will be fulfilled.

It's not going to be easy, is it?

No - his greatest challenges are ahead of him.

ON THE FIRST DAY OF THE FESTIVAL, THE DISCIPLES MADE ARRANGEMENTS, FOLLOWING JESUS' INSTRUCTIONS, TO CELEBRATE THE PASSOVER MEAL AT THE HOUSE OF A MAN IN THE CITY.

WHILE THEY WERE EATING, JESUS REVEALED THAT ONE OF THEM WOULD BETRAY HIM. JUDAS PRETENDED NOT TO KNOW ANYTHING ABOUT IT.

Take this bread and eat it; this is my body. Take this cup and drink from it, all of you. This is my blood of the covenant, which is poured out for many, for the forgiveness of sins.

JESUS TOOK SOME BREAD AND SAID A PRAYER OF THANKS. THEN HE BROKE IT AND DIVIDED IT AMONG THE DISCIPLES. NEXT HE TOOK A CUP OF WINE AND BLESSED IT. JESUS HANDED IT TO THE DISCIPLES AND THEY ALL DRANK FROM IT.

Who is it you want?

Jesus of Nazareth.

LATER THAT EVENING, JESUS LEFT WITH HIS DISCIPLES AND WENT TO THE GARDEN OF GETHSEMANE TO PRAY AND REFLECT. MUCH LATER JUDAS CAME TO THE GARDEN, TOGETHER WITH SOLDIERS FROM THE CHIEF PRIESTS AND THE PHARISEES. THEY CARRIED TORCHES, LANTERNS, AND WEAPONS.

JUDAS THEN CAME UP TO JESUS AND KISSED HIM ON THE CHEEK. THIS WAS A SIGNAL TO SHOW THE GUARDS WHICH ONE WAS JESUS.

If you are looking for me, then let these men go.

THE GUARDS STEPPED FORWARD.

Put your sword away, Peter! All those who live by the sword will die by the sword.

THEN PETER, WHO HAD A SWORD, DREW IT AND STRUCK THE HIGH PRIEST'S SERVANT, CUTTING OFF HIS RIGHT EAR. JESUS IMMEDIATELY TOLD HIM TO PUT HIS SWORD AWAY.

THEN JESUS WAS ARRESTED.

Is it true, what I hear about your disciples and your teaching?

Why are you questioning me like this? I have taught openly, hiding nothing.

PETER FOLLOWED JESUS AND THE OFFICIALS TO THE HIGH PRIEST'S HOUSE, AND WAITED OUTSIDE.

Are you the messiah, the Son of God?

It is you who say this.

18

This man has been leading our people astray by claiming he is the messiah.

JESUS WAS BROUGHT BEFORE PONTIUS PILATE, THE ROMAN GOVERNOR. THE PHARISEES BEGAN TO STATE THEIR CASE AGAINST JESUS TO THE GOVERNOR.

Are you the king of the Jews?

Does this question come from you or have other people told you about me?

PILATE TOOK JESUS INTO HIS PALACE TO QUESTION HIM.

The man has done nothing wrong!

PILATE ADDRESSED THE PRIESTS AND THE CROWD.

But his teaching causes riots wherever he goes - all over Judea, from Galilee to Jerusalem!

Well, then, send this man to Herod and let him judge whether he's guilty or innocent.

PILATE SENT JESUS TO HEROD ANTIPAS. ACCORDING TO THE LAW, GALILEE WAS UNDER HEROD'S CONTROL, AND HEROD HAPPENED TO BE IN JERUSALEM AT THE TIME.

Are you the one that can perform miracles? If you are, then do one for me. Prove to me that you're no fool.

What's wrong with him? Why isn't he answering?

HEROD WAS DELIGHTED TO MEET JESUS, BECAUSE HE HAD HEARD MUCH ABOUT HIM. HE ASKED JESUS QUESTION AFTER QUESTION, BUT JESUS REFUSED TO ANSWER. HE WAS FINALLY SENT BACK TO PILATE.

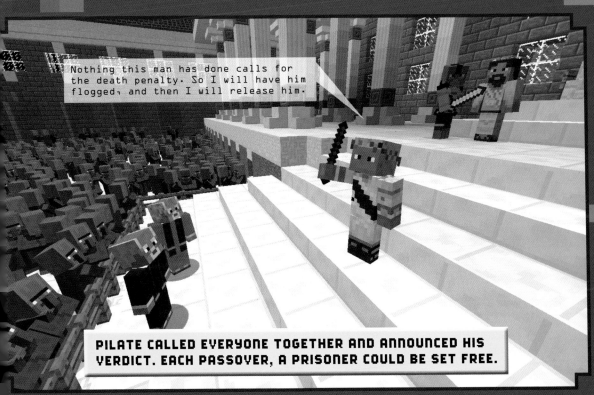

Nothing this man has done calls for the death penalty. So I will have him flogged, and then I will release him.

PILATE CALLED EVERYONE TOGETHER AND ANNOUNCED HIS VERDICT. EACH PASSOVER, A PRISONER COULD BE SET FREE.

Kill him!

Kill him!

Kill him!

Kill him!

BUT WITH ONE VOICE THE CROWD SHOUTED, "KILL HIM AND RELEASE BARABBAS!" BARABBAS HAD BEEN PUT IN PRISON FOR RIOTING AND MURDER.

23

JESUS WAS HANDED OVER TO THE ROMAN SOLDIERS. HE WAS THEN STRIPPED AND BEATEN, AND A CROWN OF THORNS WAS PLACED ON HIS HEAD.

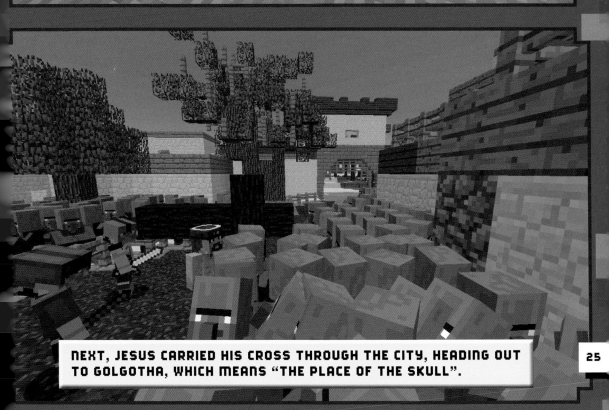

NEXT, JESUS CARRIED HIS CROSS THROUGH THE CITY, HEADING OUT TO GOLGOTHA, WHICH MEANS "THE PLACE OF THE SKULL".

AT THE EDGE OF THE CITY, JESUS COULD NO LONGER BEAR THE WEIGHT OF THE CROSS AND COLLAPSED. A MAN NAMED SIMON, WHO WAS FROM CYRENE, HAPPENED TO BE COMING IN FROM THE COUNTRYSIDE. THE SOLDIERS SEIZED HIM AND FORCED HIM TO CARRY THE CROSS INSTEAD.

OTHER CRIMINALS WERE LED OUT TO BE EXECUTED ALONG WITH JESUS. WHEN THEY CAME TO GOLGOTHA, THE SOLDIERS NAILED JESUS TO THE CROSS AND SET IT UPRIGHT. THE CRIMINALS WERE ALSO HUNG ON CROSSES — ONE TO THE RIGHT OF JESUS AND ONE TO THE LEFT.

ONE OF THE CRIMINALS HANGING BESIDE JESUS STARTED TO MOCK AND INSULT HIM, BUT THE OTHER MAN SPOKE HUMBLY.

THE DEATH AND RESURRECTION OF JESUS

Matthew 27–28; Luke 23–24

I can't look... I have to turn away.

I know. But this was all part of the plan...

Father, I entrust my spirit into your hands!

BY THIS TIME IT WAS AFTERNOON, AND DARKNESS FELL ACROSS THE WHOLE LAND. THE LIGHT FROM THE SUN WAS GONE. THEN JESUS CRIED OUT, AND WITH THOSE WORDS HE BREATHED HIS LAST LIVING BREATH.

ONE OF THE MEMBERS OF THE HIGH COUNCIL WAS A GOOD MAN NAMED JOSEPH. HE HAD NOT AGREED WITH THE DECISION OF THE OTHER RELIGIOUS LEADERS. HE WANTED JESUS' BODY TO BE TREATED WITH RESPECT, SO HE WENT TO PILATE AND ASKED FOR IT.

THEN, JOSEPH WRAPPED THE BODY IN A LONG SHEET OF LINEN CLOTH AND LAID IT IN A NEW TOMB THAT HAD BEEN CARVED OUT OF ROCK. BY NIGHTFALL, JESUS' BODY HAD BEEN PLACED INSIDE AND THE TOMB HAD BEEN SEALED, AND NOW SOLDIERS STOOD GUARD.

He's gone! All that's left is his white cloth!

How did that happen?

VERY EARLY ON SUNDAY MORNING, MARY, JESUS' MOTHER, AND MARY MAGDALENE TOOK THE SPICES THEY HAD PREPARED AND WENT TO THE TOMB. THEY WERE VERY SURPRISED TO FIND THAT THE STONE HAD BEEN ROLLED AWAY FROM THE TOMB, AND, WHEN THEY ENTERED, THEY COULD NOT SEE JESUS' BODY.

SUDDENLY, TWO MEN IN DAZZINGLY WHITE CLOTHES STOOD IN FRONT OF THEM.

It's true - Jesus has risen from the dead!

Yeah, right!

THE WOMEN RUSHED TO TELL THE DISCIPLES ALL THAT THEY HAD SEEN.

PETER RAN TO THE TOMB AND SAW THAT IT WAS EMPTY, EXCEPT FOR THE WHITE LINEN CLOTH. HE RETURNED TO THE OTHER DISCIPLES, AMAZED AT WHAT HAD HAPPENED.

JESUS IS TAKEN UP TO HEAVEN

Matthew 28; Luke 24; John 20; Acts 1

You see, I told you it would all work out.

THAT SAME DAY, TWO OF JESUS' FOLLOWERS WERE GOING TO A VILLAGE CALLED EMMAUS, ABOUT ELEVEN KILOMETRES FROM JERUSALEM. JESUS HIMSELF CAME UP AND WALKED ALONG WITH THEM, BUT THEY DID NOT RECOGNIZE HIM.

What are you discussing?

We're really sad. We thought Jesus was someone special who would change things. Some people say he's risen from the dead but we haven't seen him.

How foolish you are, and how slow to believe all that the prophets have said! Don't you see that the messiah had to suffer these things before he could enter into glory?

Please stay to eat with us, for it is already getting dark.

WHEN THEY ARRIVED AT THE VILLAGE OF EMMAUS, THE FOLLOWERS URGED JESUS TO STAY AND HAVE DINNER WITH THEM.

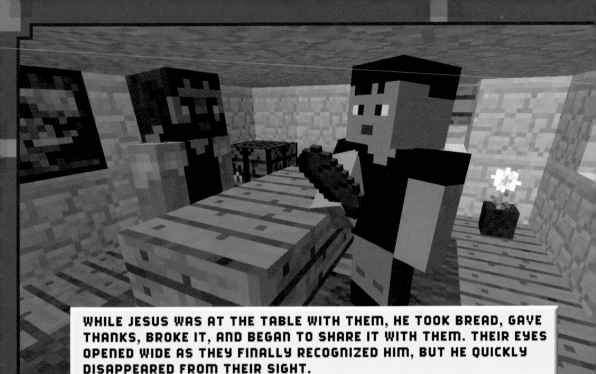

WHILE JESUS WAS AT THE TABLE WITH THEM, HE TOOK BREAD, GAVE THANKS, BROKE IT, AND BEGAN TO SHARE IT WITH THEM. THEIR EYES OPENED WIDE AS THEY FINALLY RECOGNIZED HIM, BUT HE QUICKLY DISAPPEARED FROM THEIR SIGHT.

AT ONCE, THEY RETURNED TO JERUSALEM. THERE THEY FOUND THE OTHER DISCIPLES AND TOLD THEM WHAT HAD HAPPENED.

Peace be with you.

WHILE THEY WERE TALKING ABOUT THIS, JESUS HIMSELF APPEARED AMONG THEM.

Touch me and you'll see I'm real — a ghost doesn't have flesh and bones, but I do!

THEY WERE STARTLED AND FRIGHTENED.

The Scriptures say that the messiah will suffer and rise from the dead on the third day. You have witnessed everything that has happened; and now you must tell the world about how people's sins can be forgiven. You can begin here, in Jerusalem! I am going to send you a helper, as my Father has promised.

JESUS EXPLAINED TO THE DISCIPLES HOW HIS DEATH AND RESURRECTION HAD BEEN WRITTEN ABOUT IN THE SCRIPTURES, AND THAT THEY NOW HAD A VERY IMPORTANT JOB TO DO WITH GOD'S HELP.

It is time for me to leave you. Go into the world with my blessing.

THEN JESUS TOOK HIS DISCIPLES TO BETHANY, WHERE HE LIFTED UP HIS HANDS AND BLESSED THEM.

Make people my followers wherever you go. I will always be with you.

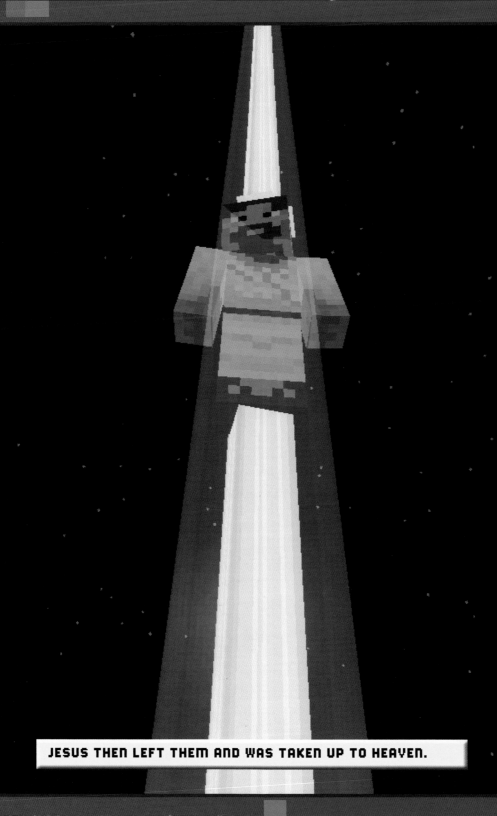

JESUS THEN LEFT THEM AND WAS TAKEN UP TO HEAVEN.

THE DISCIPLES RETURNED TO JERUSALEM AND GATHERED TOGETHER FREQUENTLY TO PRAY TO GOD.

Whoever believes in me will have eternal life.

SOON AFTER, ON THE DAY OF PENTECOST, THE DISCIPLES WERE FILLED WITH THE HOLY SPIRIT SENT BY GOD TO HELP AND ENCOURAGE THEM. AND FROM THAT DAY THEY BEGAN TO SPREAD JESUS' MESSAGE ALL AROUND THE WORLD.